LEONARD BERNSTEIN
I HATE MUSIC!
A Cycle of Five Kid Songs

CONTENTS

Edited by Richard Walters

Editorial Consultants: Marie Carter, Garth Sunderland

The Name and Likeness of "Leonard Bernstein" is a registered trademark of Amberson Holdings LLC.
Used by Permission.

ISBN 978-1-61780-486-1

LEONARD BERNSTEIN
Music Publishing
Company LLC

BOOSEY & HAWKES

AN IMAGEM COMPANY

DISTRIBUTED BY

HAL•LEONARD®
CORPORATION

7777 W. BLUEMOUND RD. P.O. BOX 13819 MILWAUKEE, WI 53213

www.leonardbernstein.com
www.boosey.com
www.halleonard.com

For Edys

I Hate Music!

A Cycle of Five Kid Songs

(In the performance of these songs, coyness is to be assiduously avoided. The natural, unforced sweetness of child expressions can never be successfully gilded; rather will it come through the music in proportion to the dignity and sophisticated understanding of the singer.)

original key

Words and Music by
LEONARD BERNSTEIN

I. My Name is Barbara

II. Jupiter Has Seven Moons

nine; _____ And

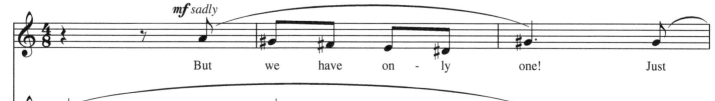

ev - 'ry one is a lit - tle sun, with six lit - tle moons of its own! _____

Molto meno mosso

mf sadly

But we have on - ly one! Just

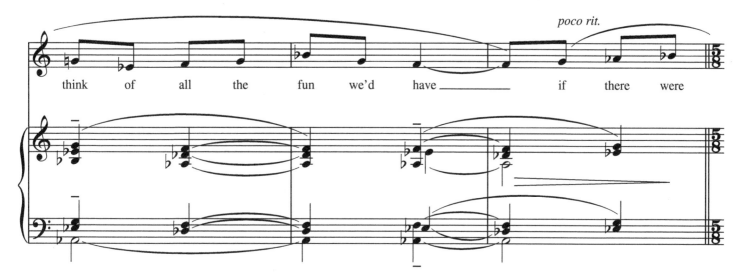

think of all the fun we'd have _____ if there were

Tempo I

nine! _____ Then

we could be _____ just nine _____ times more ro - man - tic!

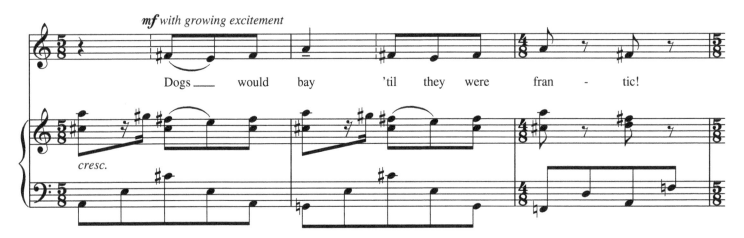

mf with growing excitement

Dogs ____ would bay 'til they were fran - tic!

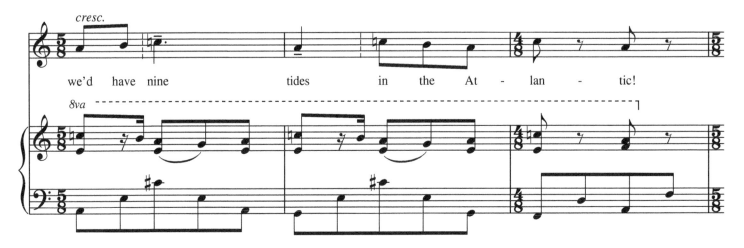

we'd have nine tides in the At - lan - tic!

The man in the moon would be gi - gan - tic!

Tempo II

But we have on - ly one!

On - ly

Tempo I

one!

III. I Hate Music!

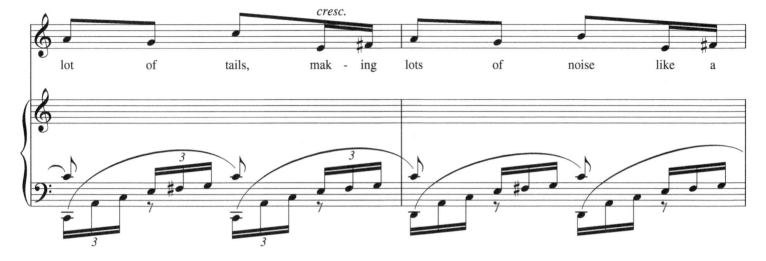

lot of tails, mak - ing lots of noise like a

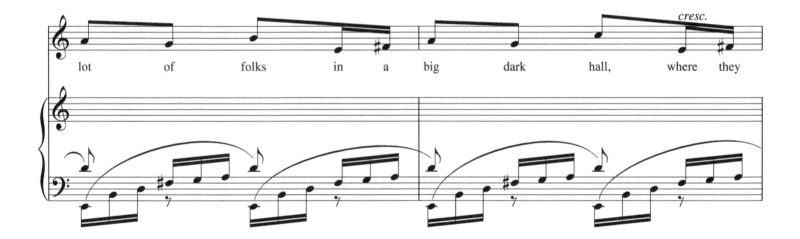

lot of fe - males; Mu - sic is a

lot of folks in a big dark hall, where they

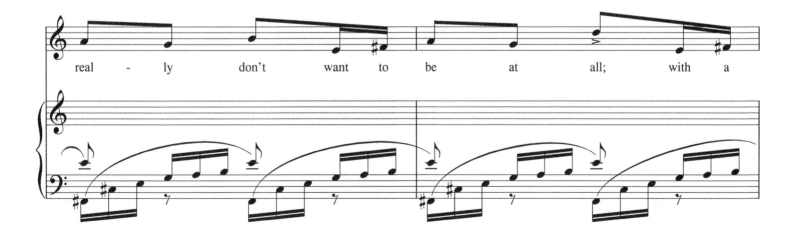

real - ly don't want to be at all; with a

IV. A Big Indian and a Little Indian

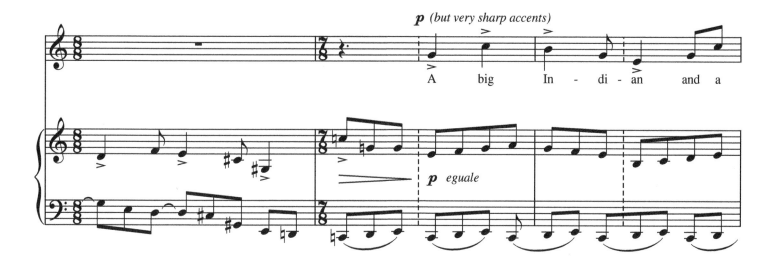

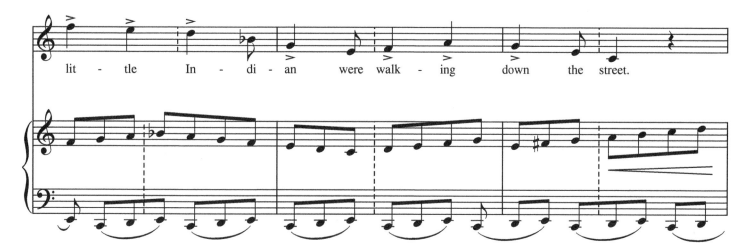

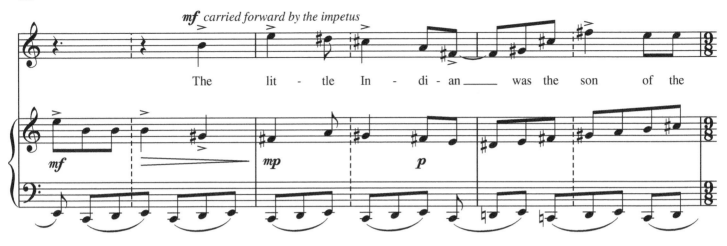

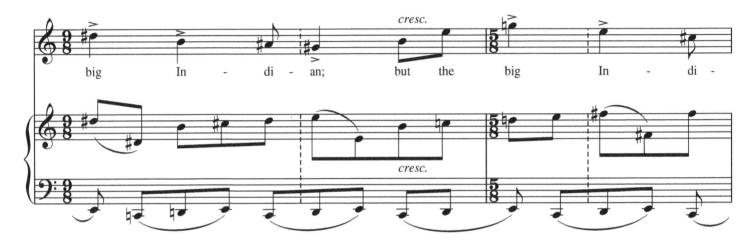

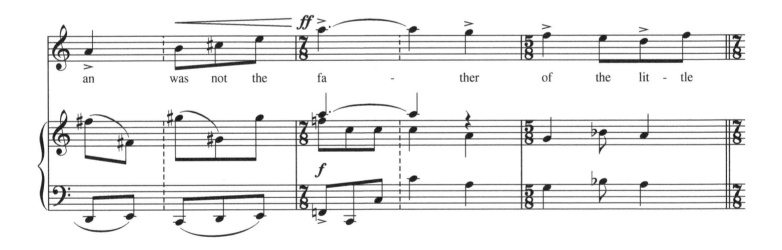

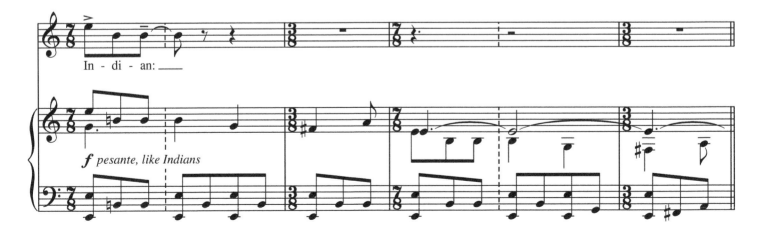

(spoken very fast)

You see the riddle is, if the little Indian
was the son of the big Indian, but the big
Indian was not the father of the little Indian,
(7) who was he?__ I'll give you two measures:

His moth - er! ____

V. I'm a Person Too

Moderato, alla marcia

I just found out to - day that I'm a per - son

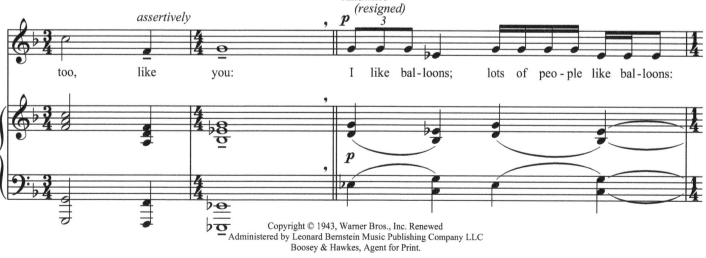

too, like you: I like bal - loons; lots of peo - ple like bal - loons:

cresc.

But ev-'ry-one says, "Is-n't she cute? She likes bal-loons!"

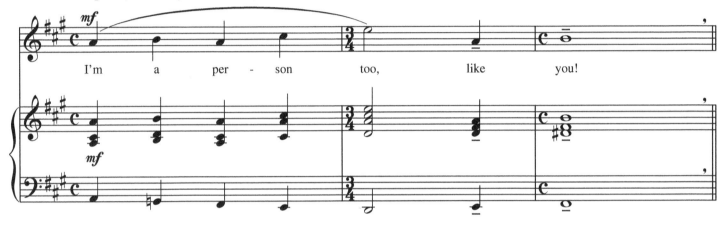

Tempo I *(recovering assertiveness)*

mf

I'm a per-son too, like you!

Tempo II *(simply, by way of explanation)*

mp   *poco accel.*

I like things that ev-'ry-one likes: I like soft things and mov-ies and hors-es and

f appealingly

warm things and red things: don't you?

Tempo I

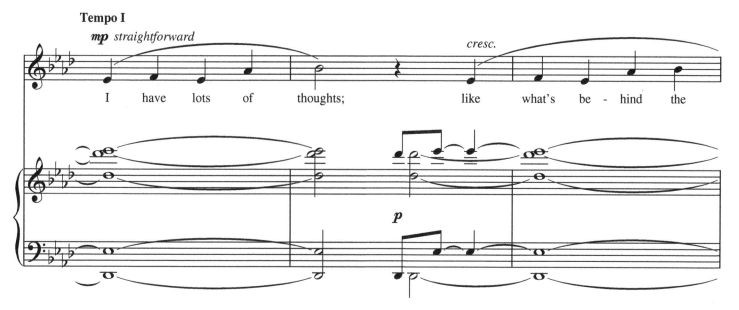

I have lots of thoughts; like what's be - hind the

sky; and what's be - hind what's be - hind the sky: But

Tempo II

ev -'ry-one says, "Is - n't she sweet? She wants to know ev -'ry-thing!" Don't you? Of

Tempo I

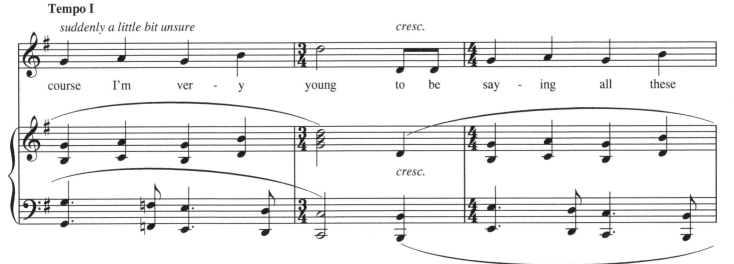

suddenly a little bit unsure   *cresc.*

course I'm ver - y young to be say - ing all these

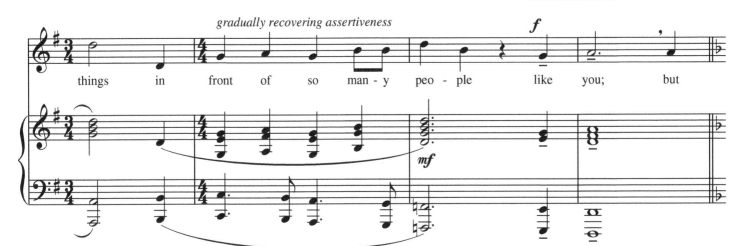

gradually recovering assertiveness

things in front of so man - y peo - ple like you; but

Meno mosso

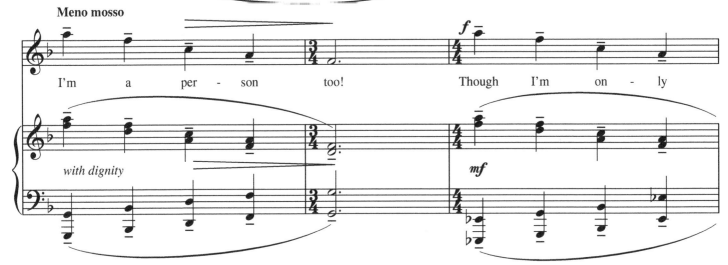

I'm a per - son too! Though I'm on - ly

with dignity

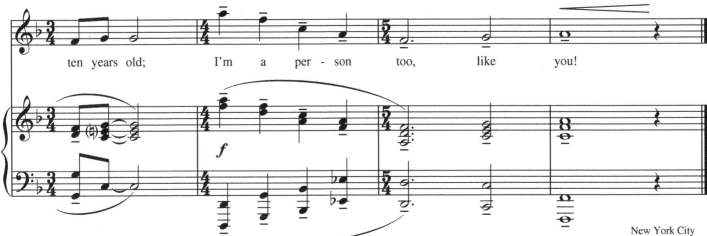

ten years old; I'm a per - son too, like you!

New York City
March, 1943